laugh

MW00721048

My Gratitude Journal

inspire

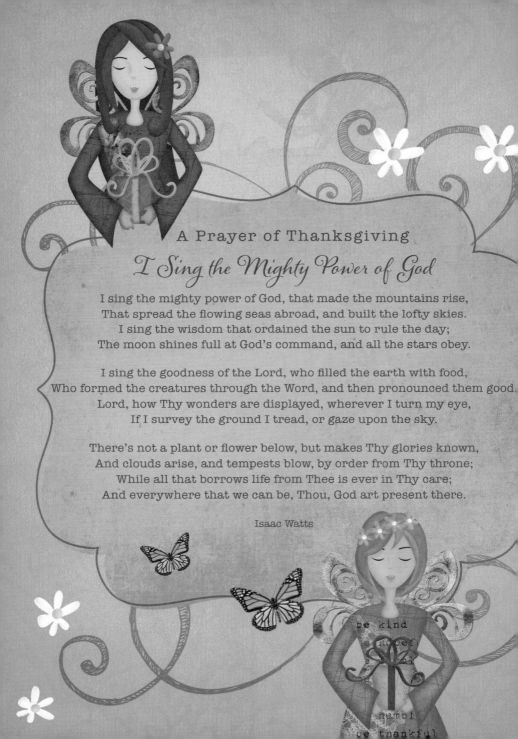

A Prayer of Thanksgiving

I Sing the Mighty Power of God

I sing the mighty power of God, that made the mountains rise,
That spread the flowing seas abroad, and built the lofty skies.
I sing the wisdom that ordained the sun to rule the day;
The moon shines full at God's command, and all the stars obey.

I sing the goodness of the Lord, who filled the earth with food,
Who formed the creatures through the Word, and then pronounced them good.
Lord, how Thy wonders are displayed, wherever I turn my eye,
If I survey the ground I tread, or gaze upon the sky.

There's not a plant or flower below, but makes Thy glories known,
And clouds arise, and tempests blow, by order from Thy throne;
While all that borrows life from Thee is ever in Thy care;
And everywhere that we can be, Thou, God art present there.

Isaac Watts

be kind

be thankful

Joy Springs from a
Grateful Heart

Our God is so great and so good!

The more we think about it the more we realize that we serve a God who deserves our praise, our adoration, our heartfelt gratitude. Not only does He provide in our daily needs and grace us with His constant presence and protection, but He has also given us the greatest Gift of all – His Son, Jesus Christ. Through Him we have life, light and love in abundance.

This journal aims to help you to take time to consciously reflect on God's blessings: His provision, His presence, His beauty seen in the everyday things around you. There are prompts in the form of Scripture verses and inspiring quotes that will help you to focus on developing an attitude of gratitude.

As you reflect on God's goodness and His blessings, you will realize that joy springs from a grateful heart. Expressing your thanks to the God who deserves our heartfelt gratitude and praise will become a source of great blessing and comfort to you.

God bless you as you live gratefully today!

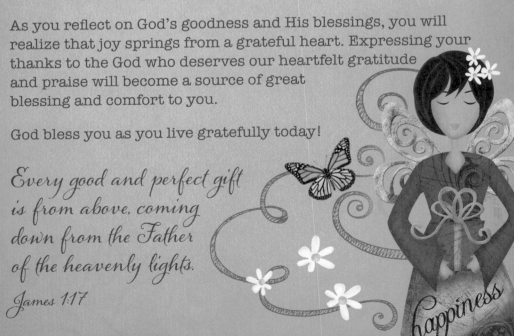

Every good and perfect gift is from above, coming down from the Father of the heavenly lights.

James 1:17

happiness

Be thankful that you don't already have everything you desire, if you did, what would there be to look forward to?

Be thankful when you don't know something, for it gives you the *opportunity* to learn.

Be thankful for the difficult times, during those times you *grow*.

Be thankful for your limitations because they give you opportunities for improvement.

Be thankful for each new challenge because it will build your *strength* and *character*

Be thankful for your mistakes, they will teach you *valuable lessons*.

Be thankful when you're tired and weary because it means you've made *a difference*.

It is easy to be thankful for the good things. A life of *rich fulfillment* comes to those who are also thankful for the setbacks.

Gratitude can turn a negative into a positive. Find a way to *be thankful* for your troubles and they can become your *blessings*.

Anonymous

Love
Live

The Lord has done *amazing* things for us!
What joy! Ps. 126:3

Gratitude can transform common days into
thanksgivings, turn routine jobs into joy,
and change ordinary opportunities into blessings.

William Arthur Ward

Thanks be to God! He gives us the victory
through our Lord Jesus Christ.
1 Cor. 15:57

The faithful *love* of the Lord never ends!

His mercies never cease. Great is His faithfulness.

Lam. 3:22-23

We are so often caught up in our destination
that we forget to appreciate the journey, especially
the *goodness* of the people we meet on the way.
Appreciation is a wonderful feeling, don't overlook it.

Anonymous

_____

_____

_____

_____

_____

_____

_____

_____

_____

_____

_____

_____

_____

_____

_____

_____

_____

_____

_____

Give *thanks* to the Lord and proclaim
His greatness. 1 Chron. 16:8

A state of mind that sees God in everything is evidence of *growth in grace* and a thankful *heart.* Charles Finney

Joy is the simplest form of *gratitude.*

Karl Barth

As we express our *gratitude*, we must never forget
that the highest appreciation is not to utter words,
but to live by them. John F. Kennedy

How *amazing* are the deeds of the Lord! Ps. 111:2

The Bible tells us that whenever we come before God,

whatever our purpose or prayer request,

we are always to come with a *thankful heart.*

David Jeremiah

Don't worry about anything; instead, pray about everything. Tell God what you need, and *thank* Him for all He has done. Phil. 4:6

Give *thanks* to the Lord, for He is good!
His faithful *love* endures forever.

1 Chron. 16:34

When you have truly thanked
the Lord for every blessing sent,
but little time will then remain
for murmur or lament.

Hannah More

I will *thank* the Lord because
He is just; I will sing praise to the name
of the Lord Most High. Ps. 7:17

O God, I will give You *thanks,* for You answered me;

You have become my salvation. Ps. 118:21

Give *thanks* for a little and you will find a lot.

Proverb

Shout for *joy* to God, all the earth!

Ps. 66:1

Give *thanks* to the Lord, for He is good!

His faithful love endures forever.

Ps. 136:1

The optimist says, the cup is half full.

The pessimist says, the cup is half empty. The child

of God says, my cup runneth over. Anonymous

Be happy! Yes, leap for joy!
For a great reward awaits you in heaven.

Luke 6:23

If the only prayer you
say in your life is thank you,
that would suffice.

Meister Eckhart

You make me *glad* by Your deeds,
Lord; I sing for *joy* at what Your
hands have done. Ps. 92:4

In Him our hearts *rejoice,* for we *trust* in His
holy name. May Your unfailing *love* be with us, Lord,
even as we put our *hope* in You. Ps. 33:21-22

God gave you a gift of 86,400 seconds today.

Have you used one to say *"thank you?"*

William Arthur Ward

Give *thanks* to the Lord and proclaim His greatness.

Let the whole world know what He has done. Ps. 105:1

God is in control, and therefore in everything I can *give thanks* – not because of the situation but because of the One who directs and rules over it. Kay Arthur

_____

_____

_____

_____

_____

_____

_____

_____

_____

_____

_____

_____

_____

_____

_____

_____

_____

Keep your face to the *sunshine* and you cannot see a shadow. Helen Keller

I am overwhelmed with *joy* in the Lord my God!
For He has dressed me with the clothing of *salvation*
and draped me in a robe of *righteousness.* Isa. 61:10

_____

_____

_____

_____

_____

_____

_____

_____

_____

_____

_____

_____

_____

_____

_____

_____

_____

_____

Never lose an opportunity of
seeing anything that is beautiful,
for beauty is God's handwriting –
a wayside sacrament. Welcome
it in every fair face, in every fair sky,
in every flower; and thank God for
it as a cup of blessing.

Ralph Waldo Emerson

You will show me the way of life,
granting me the joy of Your presence and
the pleasures of living with You forever.

Ps. 16:11

Gratitude is an offering precious in the sight of God, and it is one that the poorest of us can make and be no poorer but richer for having made it. A. W. Tozer

_____
_____
_____
_____
_____
_____
_____
_____
_____
_____
_____
_____
_____
_____

The Lord has done *amazing* things for us!
What joy! Ps. 126:3

_____

_____

_____

_____

_____

_____

_____

_____

_____

_____

_____

_____

_____

_____

_____

_____

_____

_____

_____

_____

Gratitude can transform common days into
thanksgivings, turn routine jobs into joy,
and change ordinary opportunities into blessings.

William Arthur Ward

Thanks be to God! He gives us the victory through our Lord Jesus Christ.

1 Cor. 15:57

The faithful *love* of the Lord never ends!

His mercies never cease. Great is His faithfulness.

Lam. 3:22-23

We are so often caught up in our destination
that we forget to appreciate the journey, especially
the *goodness* of the people we meet on the way.
Appreciation is a wonderful feeling, don't overlook it.

Anonymous

Give *thanks* to the Lord and proclaim His greatness. 1 Chron. 16:8

A state of mind that sees God in everything is evidence of *growth in grace* and a thankful *heart.* Charles Finney

Joy is the simplest form of *gratitude*.

Karl Barth

As we express our *gratitude,* we must never forget
that the highest appreciation is not to utter words,
but to live by them. John F. Kennedy

How *amazing* are the deeds
of the Lord! Ps. 111:2

The Bible tells us that whenever we come before God,

whatever our purpose or prayer request,

we are always to come with a *thankful heart.*

David Jeremiah

Don't worry about anything; instead,
pray about everything. Tell God what you
need, and *thank* Him for all
He has done. Phil. 4:6

Give *thanks* to the Lord, for He is good!
His faithful *love* endures forever.

1 Chron. 16:34

When you have truly thanked
the Lord for every blessing sent,
but little time will then remain
for murmur or lament.

Hannah More

I will *thank* the Lord because
He is just; I will sing praise to the name
of the Lord Most High. Ps. 7:17

O God, I will give You *thanks*, for You answered me;

You have become my salvation. Ps. 118:21

Give *thanks* for a little and you will find a lot.

Proverb

Shout for *joy* to God, all the earth!

Ps. 66:1

Give *thanks* to the Lord, for He is good!

His faithful love endures forever.

Ps. 136:1

The optimist says, the cup is half full.
The pessimist says, the cup is half empty. The child
of God says, my cup runneth over. Anonymous

Be happy! Yes, leap for joy!
For a great reward awaits you in heaven.
Luke 6:23

If the only prayer you
say in your life is thank you,
that would suffice.

Meister Eckhart

You make me *glad* by Your deeds, Lord; I sing for *joy* at what Your hands have done. Ps. 92:4

In Him our hearts *rejoice*, for we *trust* in His
holy name. May Your unfailing *love* be with us, Lord,
even as we put our *hope* in You. Ps. 33:21-22

God gave you a gift of 86,400 seconds today.

Have you used one to say *"thank you?"*

William Arthur Ward

_____

_____

_____

_____

_____

_____

_____

_____

_____

_____

_____

_____

_____

_____

_____

_____

_____

_____

Give *thanks* to the Lord and proclaim His greatness.

Let the whole world know what He has done. Ps. 105:1

God is in control, and therefore in everything I can *give thanks* – not because of the situation but because of the One who directs and rules over it. Kay Arthur

Keep your face to the *sunshine* and
you cannot see a shadow. Helen Keller

I am overwhelmed with *joy* in the Lord my God!
For He has dressed me with the clothing of *salvation*
and draped me in a robe of *righteousness.* Isa. 61:10

Never lose an opportunity of
seeing anything that is beautiful,
for beauty is God's handwriting –
a wayside sacrament. Welcome
it in every fair face, in every fair sky,
in every flower; and thank God for
it as a cup of blessing.

Ralph Waldo Emerson

You will show me the way of life,
granting me the joy of Your presence and
the pleasures of living with You forever.

Ps. 16:11

Gratitude is an offering precious in the sight of God,
and it is one that the poorest of us can make and be no poorer
but richer for having made it. A. W. Tozer

_____

_____

_____

_____

_____

_____

_____

_____

_____

_____

_____

_____

_____

_____

The Lord has done *amazing* things for us!

What joy! Ps. 126:3

Gratitude can transform common days into
thanksgivings, turn routine jobs into joy,
and change ordinary opportunities into blessings.

William Arthur Ward

Thanks be to God! He gives us the victory through our Lord Jesus Christ.

1 Cor. 15:57

The faithful *love* of the Lord never ends!

His mercies never cease. Great is His faithfulness.

Lam. 3:22-23

We are so often caught up in our destination
that we forget to appreciate the journey, especially
the *goodness* of the people we meet on the way.
Appreciation is a wonderful feeling, don't overlook it.

Anonymous

Give *thanks* to the Lord and proclaim

His greatness. 1 Chron. 16:8

A state of mind that sees God in everything is evidence of *growth in grace* and a thankful *heart.* Charles Finney

Joy is the simplest form of *gratitude.*
Karl Barth

As we express our *gratitude,* we must never forget
that the highest appreciation is not to utter words,
but to live by them. John F. Kennedy

How *amazing* are the deeds
of the Lord! Ps. 111:2

The Bible tells us that whenever we come before God,

whatever our purpose or prayer request,

we are always to come with a *thankful heart.*

David Jeremiah

Don't worry about anything; instead, pray about everything. Tell God what you need, and *thank* Him for all He has done. Phil. 4:6

Give *thanks* to the Lord, for He is good!
His faithful *love* endures forever.

1 Chron. 16:34

When you have truly thanked
the Lord for every blessing sent,
but little time will then remain
for murmur or lament.

Hannah More

I will *thank* the Lord because
He is just; I will sing praise to the name
of the Lord Most High. Ps. 7:17

O God, I will give You *thanks,* for You answered me;

You have become my salvation. Ps. 118:21

Give *thanks* for a little and you will find a lot.

Proverb

Shout for *joy* to God, all the earth!

Ps. 66:1

Give *thanks* to the Lord, for He is good!

His faithful love endures forever.

Ps. 136:1

The optimist says, the cup is half full.

The pessimist says, the cup is half empty. The child

of God says, my cup runneth over. Anonymous

Be happy! Yes, leap for joy!
For a great reward awaits you in heaven.
Luke 6:23

_____
_____
_____
_____
_____
_____
_____
_____
_____
_____
_____
_____
_____
_____

If the only prayer you say in your life is thank you, that would suffice.

Meister Eckhart

You make me *glad* by Your deeds,
Lord; I sing for *joy* at what Your
hands have done. Ps. 92:4

In Him our hearts *rejoice,* for we *trust* in His
holy name. May Your unfailing *love* be with us, Lord,
even as we put our *hope* in You. Ps. 33:21-22

God gave you a gift of 86,400 seconds today.

Have you used one to say *"thank you?"*

William Arthur Ward

Give *thanks* to the Lord and proclaim His greatness.

Let the whole world know what He has done. Ps. 105:1

God is in control, and therefore in everything I can *give thanks* – not because of the situation but because of the One who directs and rules over it. Kay Arthur

Keep your face to the *sunshine* and
you cannot see a shadow. Helen Keller

I am overwhelmed with *joy* in the Lord my God!
For He has dressed me with the clothing of *salvation*
and draped me in a robe of *righteousness*. Isa. 61:10

Never lose an opportunity of
seeing anything that is beautiful,
for beauty is God's handwriting –
a wayside sacrament. Welcome
it in every fair face, in every fair sky,
in every flower; and thank God for
it as a cup of blessing.

Ralph Waldo Emerson

You will show me the way of life,
granting me the joy of Your presence and
the pleasures of living with You forever.

Ps. 16:11

Gratitude is an offering precious in the sight of God, and it is one that the poorest of us can make and be no poorer but richer for having made it. A. W. Tozer

_____

_____

_____

_____

_____

_____

_____

_____

_____

_____

_____

_____

_____

_____

_____

The Lord has done *amazing* things for us!
What joy! Ps. 126:3

Gratitude can transform common days into
thanksgivings, turn routine jobs into joy,
and change ordinary opportunities into blessings.
William Arthur Ward

Thanks be to God! He gives us the victory through our Lord Jesus Christ.

1 Cor. 15:57

The faithful *love* of the Lord never ends!

His mercies never cease. Great is His faithfulness.

Lam. 3:22-23

We are so often caught up in our destination
that we forget to appreciate the journey, especially
the *goodness* of the people we meet on the way.
Appreciation is a wonderful feeling, don't overlook it.

Anonymous

_____

_____

_____

_____

_____

_____

_____

_____

_____

_____

_____

_____

_____

Give *thanks* to the Lord and proclaim

His greatness. 1 Chron. 16:8

A state of mind that sees God in everything is evidence of *growth in grace* and a thankful *heart.* Charles Finney

Joy is the simplest form of *gratitude.*
Karl Barth

As we express our *gratitude*, we must never forget
that the highest appreciation is not to utter words,
but to live by them. John F. Kennedy

How *amazing* are the deeds
of the Lord! Ps. 111:2

The Bible tells us that whenever we come before God,

whatever our purpose or prayer request,

we are always to come with a *thankful heart.*

David Jeremiah

Don't worry about anything; instead,
pray about everything. Tell God what you
need, and *thank* Him for all
He has done. Phil. 4:6

Give *thanks* to the Lord, for He is good!
His faithful *love* endures forever.

1 Chron. 16:34

When you have truly thanked
the Lord for every blessing sent,
but little time will then remain
for murmur or lament.

Hannah More

I will *thank* the Lord because
He is just; I will sing praise to the name
of the Lord Most High. Ps. 7:17

O God, I will give You *thanks,* for You answered me;

You have become my salvation. Ps. 118:21

Give *thanks* for a little and you will find a lot.

Proverb

Shout for *joy* to God, all the earth!

Ps. 66:1

Give *thanks* to the Lord, for He is good!

His faithful love endures forever.

Ps. 136:1

The optimist says, the cup is half full.

The pessimist says, the cup is half empty. The child

of God says, my cup runneth over. Anonymous

Be happy! Yes, leap for joy!
For a great reward awaits you in heaven.
Luke 6:23

_____

_____

_____

_____

_____

_____

_____

_____

_____

_____

_____

_____

_____

_____

_____

If the only prayer you say in your life is thank you, that would suffice.

Meister Eckhart

You make me *glad* by Your deeds, Lord; I sing for *joy* at what Your hands have done. Ps. 92:4

_____

_____

_____

_____

_____

_____

_____

_____

_____

_____

_____

_____

_____

_____

_____

_____

_____

_____

_____

In Him our hearts *rejoice*, for we *trust* in His
holy name. May Your unfailing *love* be with us, Lord,
even as we put our *hope* in You. Ps. 33:21-22

God gave you a gift of 86,400 seconds today.

Have you used one to say *"thank you?"*

William Arthur Ward

_____

_____

_____

_____

_____

_____

_____

_____

_____

_____

_____

_____

_____

_____

_____

_____

_____

_____

Give *thanks* to the Lord and proclaim His greatness.

Let the whole world know what He has done. Ps. 105:1

God is in control, and therefore in everything I can *give thanks* – not because of the situation but because of the One who directs and rules over it. Kay Arthur

_____

_____

_____

_____

_____

_____

_____

_____

_____

_____

_____

_____

_____

_____

_____

Keep your face to the *sunshine* and

you cannot see a shadow. Helen Keller

I am overwhelmed with *joy* in the Lord my God!
For He has dressed me with the clothing of *salvation*
and draped me in a robe of *righteousness*. Isa. 61:10

_____

_____

_____

_____

_____

_____

_____

_____

_____

_____

_____

_____

_____

_____

_____

_____

_____

Never lose an opportunity of
seeing anything that is beautiful,
for beauty is God's handwriting –
a wayside sacrament. Welcome
it in every fair face, in every fair sky,
in every flower; and thank God for
it as a cup of blessing.

Ralph Waldo Emerson

You will show me the way of life,
granting me the joy of Your presence and
the pleasures of living with You forever.

Ps. 16:11

Gratitude is an offering precious in the sight of God, and it is one that the poorest of us can make and be no poorer but richer for having made it. A. W. Tozer

_____

_____

_____

_____

_____

_____

_____

_____

_____

_____

_____

_____

_____